**NATIONAL
GEOGRAPHIC**

T0052137

How We Learn About Space

Andrew Einspruch

Contents

This boy is taking a closer ▶
look at the night sky.

What's in Space?

Take a look at the night sky. What do you see? You might see the moon and some stars. You might even see a planet. People have always wanted to learn about things in the night sky.

There are lots of ways to learn about something. You can look at it closely. You can touch it. You can run tests. But how do you do this when the thing you want to learn about is millions of miles away?

Telescopes

One way to study space is to look at it. Using just your eyes, you can see many things in the night sky. You can see the moon, lots of stars, and some of the planets. If you want a better look, you need to use a **telescope**.

Telescopes: Big and Small

A telescope lets you look closely at things that are far away. A simple telescope is a tube with a large piece of curved glass at one end and a smaller piece of curved glass at the other. With a small telescope you can see craters on the moon.

The moon looks bigger and ▶ closer through a telescope.

Not all telescopes are small. Some telescopes are so big they need their own special buildings. These special buildings are called **observatories**. Scientists use big telescopes to study faraway planets and stars.

Scientists open the roof on ▶ an observatory when they use the telescope.

The Hubble Space Telescope

There can be problems with using telescopes on Earth. Clouds, dirty air, and city lights get in the way of seeing objects in space. To get around this problem, scientists built a space telescope.

The Hubble Space Telescope was sent into space in 1990. It **orbits**, or travels around, Earth. Hubble orbits about 350 miles above Earth where there aren't any lights or dirty air.

Hubble sends pictures of space back to Earth. Scientists have seen amazing things in these pictures. They saw a comet crash into Jupiter. They also discovered small moons that circle Saturn and Uranus.

Hubble is released from ▶ the spacecraft that carried it into space.

◀ This picture of Mars was taken by Hubble.

Hubble Facts

✳ Hubble is about the size of a bus. It weighs about the same as two full-grown elephants.

✳ It takes 97 minutes for Hubble to orbit Earth. It travels 5 miles every second.

Sending People Into Space

If you are curious about a country, you can read about it and look at pictures. But to find out what it is really like, you have to go there. It's the same with space. The best way to get to know it is to go there.

The First Person in Space

People started traveling into space in 1961. Yuri Gagarin, the Russian **astronaut**, was the first human to go into space. He orbited Earth once.

The first spacecraft was blasted into space on powerful rockets. The first astronauts spent time learning how to live in space without **gravity**. Gravity is a strong force that pulls things toward Earth.

▲ Yuri Gagarin went into space on Apr 12, 1961.

▲ Astronauts float in space because there is no gravity there.

Going to the Moon

The moon is the closest thing in space to Earth. It is much closer than the sun or the planets. Scientists sent astronauts to the moon so they could learn what it was like there.

Before going to the moon, American astronauts made ten trips into space. These flights tested ideas about getting to the moon and back. Finally, in 1969, two astronauts landed on the moon. Neil Armstrong and Edwin "Buzz" Aldrin collected moon rocks to bring back to Earth.

◀ Buzz Aldrin walked on the moon on July 20, 1969.

The last time people went to the moon was 1972. Two astronauts drove around in a moon car called a lunar rover. They drove about 20 miles. They collected 243 pounds of rocks from many different places.

▼ An astronaut drives the lunar rover on the moon.

Space Stations

Space stations are places where people can live in space. Space stations orbit around Earth. Crews of astronauts live in space stations for many months at a time.

International Space Station

Sixteen countries worked together to create the International Space Station, or ISS. The first parts of the ISS were sent into space in 1998. People first lived in the International Space Station in 2000.

The ISS was made in large pieces called **modules**. The modules were sent into space one at a time. Then they were put together there. People live and work in one of the modules. Another module is a **laboratory.** Scientific experiments are done there.

Astronauts from different countries work in the ISS.

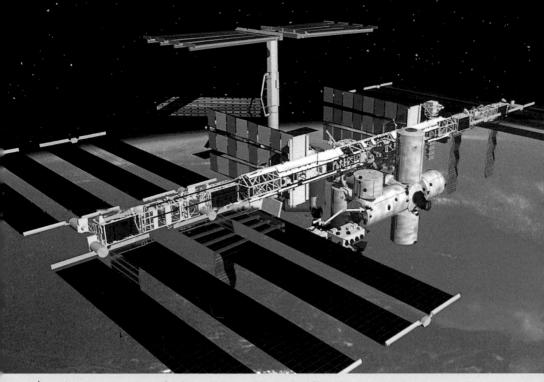

▲ The pieces of the International Space Station were put together in space.

Space Station Facts

✳ The ISS orbits 250 miles above Earth.
✳ Scientists in the ISS are learning how people can live without gravity.

Living in Space

People in space need to do the same everyday things that you need to do. They need to eat and drink. They also need to exercise their bodies so that they stay healthy.

Astronauts living in the space station eat three meals every day. Some foods, like nuts and fruit, are the same as we eat on Earth. Other foods are dried so they weigh less and can be stored longer. Foods are stored in packages that hold enough for one meal.

All astronauts exercise for at least one hour each day. The space station has exercise equipment that helps astronauts exercise all of their muscles. There is a machine that the astronauts use to strengthen their arms. There is also a machine for walking.

▲ Food for the astronauts is stored in packages.

This astronaut ▶
uses a machine to
exercise his legs.

Science in Space

The International Space Station is a great place for science. Scientists can look down on Earth and study its weather. From space, it is easy to watch how clouds move around the planet.

Scientists in the ISS study how things live without gravity. For example, scientists look at what happens to people's bodies when they spend a lot of time in space. If astronauts don't exercise, they find it hard to walk when they get back to Earth.

Scientists also do experiments on plants in the space station. They look at how plants grow without gravity. This helps them figure out if astronauts will be able to grow their own food one day.

▲ This scientist is doing an experiment to grow plants in space.

◀ Scientists in the space station can see clouds moving around Earth.

17

Space Probes

Astronauts haven't been to the planets because they are so far away from Earth. So scientists send **space probes** to planets to get a closer look. Space probes are unmanned spacecraft.

The First Space Probes

The first space probes were sent into space about 50 years ago. They were sent to the moon, Venus, and Mars. Since then, space probes have visited every planet except Pluto.

Using space probes, scientists have seen lightning and storms on Jupiter. They have discovered that Saturn has over 1,000 rings. They have also seen pictures of clouds on Neptune.

◀ The red spot on Jupiter is a never-ending storm.

◀ This space probe sends photos of planets back to Earth.

Space Probe Facts

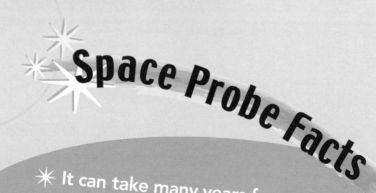

✳ It can take many years for a space probe to reach a distant planet.

✳ Jupiter: 2 years

✳ Saturn: 4 years

✳ Uranus: $8\frac{1}{2}$ years

✳ Neptune: 12 years

Exploring Mars

Some space probes land on a planet. In 2004, two space probes called rovers landed on Mars. The rovers were robots on wheels. They explored Mars and sent information back to Earth.

▼ The rover sent information about Mars back to Earth.

The rovers took color pictures of Mars. The pictures showed the rocks, craters, and red soil on Mars. The rovers also drilled into rocks. The rovers had tools to help scientists learn more about the rocks on Mars.

The rovers found ice on Mars. The ice is made from water. Finding water on Mars makes scientists wonder if there was life on this planet at one time.

◀ A photo taken by one of the rovers shows the planet's red, rocky surface.

Looking Ahead

We know a lot about space, but there is much more to learn. Scientists have lots of ideas. Some want to go back to the moon. Others want to send people to Mars. One thing is certain. People will always look up into the night sky and want to know more about what's out there.

▼ These people are using telescopes to look at the stars.

Glossary

astronaut   a person trained to fly a spacecraft

gravity   a force that pulls things toward Earth

laboratory   a place where experiments are done

module   a part that fits with other parts to make something

observatory   a building with a powerful telescope for observing the sky

orbit   to travel in a curved path around a planet or star

space probe   unmanned spacecraft that travels in space to collect information about space and send it back to Earth

telescope   an instrument that makes distant objects look closer and bigger

Index